ECHO OF HUMANITY

Adele Mourad

authorHOUSE®

AuthorHouse™
1663 Liberty Drive
Bloomington, IN 47403
www.authorhouse.com
Phone: 1-800-839-8640

First published by AuthorHouse 06/27/2011

ISBN: 978-1-4520-9738-1 (sc)
ISBN: 978-1-4520-9739-8 (e)

Library of Congress Control Number: 2010918986

Printed in the United States of America

This book is printed on acid-free paper.

Certain stock imagery © Thinkstock.

Dedication

To each member of my family (my father, mother and siblings), I dedicate *Echo of Humanity*.

To my mother Laurice T. Mourad, who still blesses my life with her presence amongst us and who nurtured my heart with her exemplary devotion, her unrelenting optimism, and her outpouring boost and encouragement.

To my siblings, who each in their own individuality bonded under the umbrella of love and grew in the strength of mutual respect and appreciation for one another.

Each one of my siblings deserves mention: my brother Tony and his fatherly care; my sister Dunia and her commendable commitment and sacrifices; my brother Michael's unyielding support, his wife Caroline who brought us joy with their three angels, Georges, Amia-Laurice, and Anthony, for whom I live and breathe and whose smiles have redefined my life and whose love has redesigned my future.

A unique class of thanks is expressed to my father, Georges T. Mourad, who has been and will remain my inspiration before and after his death. His mentorship, his scholarly guidance, his saintly love for us, and his friendship will forever proliferate in the fabric of my everyday life.

Special thanks to all my friends and acquaintances, so many they are, I offer thanks for their friendship and their warm welcome of me into their lives.

CONTENTS

INTRODUCTION

As we transition into evolving eras of modernization, technological inventions, development, and change, there has been a noted concern in humanity coping with the speed of time and changes without loosing its core essence of civilization.

The human advances have erroneously reaffirmed in some of us a conceited belief in the invincibility of the human mind on earth. The intervention of superior guidance of morals, ethics, and higher ideals in our lives have lost their significance as unnecessary, obsolete, and outdated.

Yet, the magical question on life remains: its meaning and purpose, creating a vacuum within the self, leaving a sharp feeling of loneliness, emptiness, and incompleteness in spite of all the magic the modern world has brought.

Within this context, *Echo of Humanity* highlights the

value of sustenance to ideals and the significance of allowing the intervention of mainstream ethics and morals into the simplicity of our day-to-day existence while we embrace progress and modernization.

The core message of the book is not intended to punish us for our mistakes, because we are all human and prone to error more than few times in our lifetimes. It also doesn't diminish the value of progress and developments. Instead, *Echo of Humanity* explores the opportune instances when we drift from the essential component of our humanity. It furthers emphasizes the freedom of will we individuals enjoy in allowing or repelling the intervention of good mainstream ethics and values into the making of our own choices. In doing so, it links the role of superior values, beliefs, and ethics to the meaning and purpose of existence in all of its divisions and subdivisions of life, death, infinity, and beyond.

All of this is put in a quick-to-read layout with a simple and unique freestyle of writing that is graceful in format. This style renders the book engaging, immensely fulfilling, and most relaxing.

CHAPTER ONE

A SPIRIT IN TURMOIL

*"He who wants eternity must glorify his soul
"and raise it above the needs of man
for he who is human is God first."*

How many years have I spent searching for knowledge? How many months have I endured trying to touch the realities that shape my existence? I leave my belongings, close my door, and walk away toward the unknown. I pass through the ages, crossing immense distances of many centuries. With me travels a disturbing feeling of fear that shakes me up from the peace of loneliness.

Upon arrival, the sun of the morning spring shines with delight and splendor. No man can describe the beauty of this land! No man can describe how the grace of the angels caresses one's soul and how the chanting of their psalms perfumes one's sins. And I kneel humble to the ground at the sight of the divine world of truth, kissing the land that the holy hands of wisdom have designed. And I walk alone in the paradise of the gods, yet I feel no solitude! I hear the welcoming prayers of my friends. I sense the warmth of their hands touch mine. I feel their smiles fall upon my presence like the sweet kiss of the morning dew falls upon the tender petal of the wild rose.

I who wept upon departure no longer suffer the pain of departure. I whose love for my siblings nurtured my days and cleansed my nights no longer ache over the days of departure. I who prayed to the saints of the heavens on the loving bosom of my mother and learned the book of life by the passionate care of my father no longer cry over the cruel distances that separate us. I am the fortunate who wanders in the land beyond, singing the song of thanks and shedding the tears of happiness. But why do I weep so vehemently as I look behind and long for angelic moments that my dears and I lived together? Why does melancholy still envelop me each time I look behind? Why do I remain fearful yet brave, perplexed yet enlightened, and lonesome yet rejoiced each time I recollect the instances of the past? A secret that forever shadows our existences each time destiny meets life, but my voyage will not unravel.

* * * * * * * * * * * *

Suddenly, a loud voice of wailing breaks into the silence of my meditation. Right by me stands a disturbed and sad man, chained by millions and millions of thoughts. There he is crying and struggling against an invisible being that neither he nor I can see. I ask him with great concern, "Who are you, my friend, and whom are you warring with?" "I am the unfortunate man of this world", he says, "a vicious being captured me and threw me into this foreign land away from my home and my fortune. I want to go back lest my friends and my enemies partake of my possessions."

I remain silent for a moment, trying to find a way to help this restless man until a cool breeze passes us sending gentle cheers to our innermost. Up above I see a magnificent white horse flying the skies of immortality, carrying on its back the secret of existence. It lands by us, flapping its white wings with majestic holiness. On its back the king of all kings steps down, while the angels with all the creatures of this world kneel down to him with awe and respect. And the bliss of his presence overwhelms me, yet I see not his face!

His crown is gilded with authority.

His robe is woven with the threads of eternity.

He stands high and loftily, yet his voice reveals all humility.

And the eyes of wisdom smile with pride at the sight of her beloved son.

Then the angry man looks at the king and says: "Who are you miserable creature, and why do you haunt me? They call you king, and I see not your crown! You are no royalty to me!"

The king looks at the man and says: "I am the impetus of life and the beauty of death.

"I am the light that you failed to see. I am the splendor that you could not enjoy.

"I am the happiness that you refused to feel. My essence is in you, but yours is in the midst of greed, the evil of all evils.

"I am the one who watched you in your lonesome nights kneel at the steps of my holy temple. And in your sunny bright mornings, I saw you give your heart offerings to the god of your fortune.

"I am the one who ached when I felt the unrest of your soul. In the golden corners of your palace, I pitied you warring with yourself, chained by your own corrupt thoughts.

"There by your fortune and here in the heart of the kingdom of peace you remain unable to find solace!

"I gave you my cup to drink the water of life, but under your feet you crushed the cup and kept thirsty for water.

"I gave you my hand to lean on, but with your own sword you cut off the hand and forever remained in search of love and compassion.

"You swore the truth by my name, and then you reviled my name and the name of my forefathers.

"I am the truth! Through me you see your own truth! With my seed you plant your own fruit!

"He who seeks not my truth finds nothing but darkness and hears nothing but teeth grinding. He who plants not my seed harvests nothing but drought and hunger.

"Like a blind man, he is in a vast sea. He embarks his ship toward the Promised Land, but instead he sails adrift in the midst of the continent, forever wandering with no destination or rest.

"I am the son of humanity. You are the son of earthly treasures. Your god is my enemy. Your prayers are my deception.

"Look at the abundance of my fruitful orchards; they secure man's needs! Feel the fertility of my sacred soil; it restores man's beliefs. Open your eyes and look onto me, for here in my midst the rich and the poor dine together at the table of love. Look back and see what becomes of your fortune. See how in the blink of an eye your treasure turns into ashes.

"Thus your soul, like ashes, shall wander in the abyss of earth. For there, you have implanted your endeavors, and on those ashes you have built your eternal kingdom."

* * * * * * * * * * * *

Then, a loud thunder shakes the consonance of the land. Dark clouds embrace the space in its entirety. In the center glimmers a golden cup. On its edges fall the tears of humanity. From its mouth cries the voice of wisdom. And I stand, taken aback by the discoveries of my voyage. And I praise God numerous times as I march toward the world of truth. On my side flickers the light of knowledge. Ahead of me shines the secret of existence. And in my heart pounds the passion of my beloved ones. As I walk further, I see my family assembling joyfully. I see my shadow entertaining their spirits. I see all of our souls dancing harmoniously to the songs of life. And I hear the angels chanting the holy anthem of wisdom:

"He who wants wealth must remain poor.

"He who wants love must discover hatred, for there hatred lies in the abyss of his own corruption.

"He who wants knowledge must light his own candle,

for there knowledge lies in the darkness of his own ignorance.

"He who wants truth must rise above the realities beneath him, for truth lies in the whole sum of existence and beyond.

"He who wants eternity must glorify his soul and raise it above the needs of man for he who is human is God first."

And the secret forever shadowing our existence each time destiny meets life has unraveled itself, adding a new dimension to a voyage destined to infinity.

CHAPTER TWO

SODOM AND GOMORRAH

"What becomes of love when it loses sanctity?"
"What becomes of men when they lose their souls?"

A companion whom I've missed for ages greets me with tears of love and respect. I ask: "Have you found what you were looking for?" Companion with sorrow and regrets recounts its mystical search....

"I find myself," says companion, "in a city during the late twentieth century that uniquely has no gate through which one could enter or an exit from which one could escape. Incapable of distinguishing between dream and reality, I wander in the corners of this world, lost in the sparkles of a technological era. He who invents such marvels, I say, is truly a genius! I walk into a store, and at my steps, the door opens like magic!

Doors open and close without being pushed or pulled. Money transactions take place through a machine. Cash bursts out at a push button. People of this planet have reached the moon and many other planets beyond. Their minds invade the unknown, the luminous space and stars.

Unexpectedly, a deep and proprietary voice exclaims: *Civilization.*

In this glorious age, I am told, the genius of an incredible physician produces babies in tubes. Couples will no longer suffer deprivation from the joyous gift of parenthood. Now, they shall rejoice over the gifts of time.

The same voice I hear again echoing from the skies above: *Science.*

I walk farther; I encounter men and women mingling in the streets with fascinating multicolored hair. I see men wearing earrings and all the jewelry a girl's heart desires. I walk by an agglomerate of ladies, marching in the corner, half naked, proud, and ecstatic. The same mysterious voice cries: *Modernization.*

I notice men with ponytails, gallivanting comfortably throughout the city. I notice others with one side of their heads shaved and more with both sides shaved, leaving only a hair line in the middle. They look at me with the most relaxed smile I have ever seen on a man's face.

The same extraordinary voice whispers: *Fashion.*

I learn of a mother who shoots her children to death! They talk about a father who abuses and rapes his children! I read about an eighty-year-old woman who was raped and killed and then had her golden teeth stolen! Then I hear the majestic bells of freedom tolling in the spacious courts of laws and justice.

I learn of the many who no longer believe in the sacraments of marriage. In modern days, old religious values lose their meaning. God the Almighty is a fiction invented by the imagination of superstitious men.

Liberalism, the fatherly voice exclaims.

On this planet, I am told, a person's substance is in how much wealth he gathers. The heart, the soul, and the spirit; the pursuit of the highest ideals; the significance of ethics and nobility; and all that upgrade men into the climax of humanity matter no more. He who has no money has no worth. And he who lives in the century must belong; otherwise, he will be caste ancient and obsolete, traditionalist, and unadventurous. Being a progressive liberal now translates into the rebellious dissenter.

The powerful mind that explores space and its avenues

can no longer maintain the aura of humanity that distinguishes men from beasts and that betters humans over one another.

Humanity ridicules its own essence. And I feel alone, crushed to my innermost!

In the midst of lost generations whose paths are only a rebellion against nature, I address wisdom with reverence and pain.

What becomes of salt when it loses flavor?

What becomes of honey when it loses sweetness?

What becomes of magnet when it loses force?

What becomes of love when it loses sanctity?

What becomes of candles when they bear no more light?

What becomes of men when they lose their souls?

What happened to the children of those who long ago edified Plato and Aristotle, praised Beethoven and Bach, lauded Michael Angelo and El Greco, and glorified Peter the Great and Napoleon? Now they extol money and its gifts? Now they endear lust and abhor love? Does eternity stem from earthly kingdoms filled with materialistic joy?

Does heaven hide in the corners of those extravagant palaces garnished with red carpets and golden doors? Do hell and repentance lie in those miserable cold corners where men, envious of their brothers, revile existence in greed and anger?

And suddenly, like in a miraculous moment, I find myself out of this tragedy. An enormous power shakes me up from the pains of reality. Solace befalls my trembling heart. I kneel and thank the graceful arm that saved me from the abyss of fire.

The same voice that haunts me throughout utters to my ears as such: *There you are, out of a being, and onto your own being you shall return, for you have chosen to remain in search of the civilization of the children of god!"*

On this note companion ends the recital..

CHAPTER THREE

MEN OF VIRTUE

"Is there life without challenge?"
"Is there victory without risks?"
"Is there power without bravery?"

Shadow of the Light

It is autumn, and the colorful leaves are gracefully falling and harmoniously dancing with the moves of the soft breeze. Here lies a world of beauty where nature is only a reflection of the wonders of God. The mountains and their secrets, the plains and their fertility, and the oceans and their mystery all reveal a painting of a magnificent reality of life on earth.

Walking in this heavenly piece of land, a beautiful scent of wild roses pulls me into a hidden road. I follow the magical aroma passing through the thick fog where mystical calmness reigns. I recall the voice of the centuries calling me; "Finally the time has come," the voice says, "when one must take the imminent trip into the world of discovery. An esoteric voyage it is through which one must learn what makes humanity worthy of the beatitude of life." Taken away by so many thoughts, I forget the reality of the present.

* * * * * * * * * * * *

Suddenly I find myself facing an old and antiquated palace. On its top rises a majestic dome glorified in color and architecture.

Around its shiny walls a cluster of white doves flies just like angels fly at the gates of heaven! At the main entrance, a dozen white columns stand, colossal in height and massive in width. Around them a large crowd gathers with praises and cheers for the royal wedding. I walk through, enthused by the festive sound of lyres and cymbals, enthused indeed by the beautiful wall inscriptions adorning the corridors of the saintly palace. There are thousands of psalms that one could find carved by the hearts of those men who went looking for the light—those who lost their gods and those who lost their souls and so many more that lost their virtues.

On my way to find God I kneel and pray to cleanse my soul. I repent. I sob. Nature with me weeps, and the years of my life roll.

Spring comes, and winter goes, yet my heart is in pain.

Summer opens its happy doors, yet my sins there remain.

In autumn I decide to leave and run away from all that reminds me of the horrors of the past.

I reach the desert after an endless march. I see darkness shedding its dusky veil, drawing a gigantic and fearful arch.

There I call God in poetry, in songs, and in wails until the silence of the desert breaks, and a voice of authority and kindness prevails. From beyond the arch it flows and utters the most mysterious words:

"Remember," says the voice, *"that he who reigns in the highest court of ethics is the truth that you shall always seek."*

"It is he who carries the torch of all virtues, the light that kindles the flame of eternity.

Follow the flame of your soul. You shall find the light; for in the center of mankind the torch of humanity is lit."

Endless tales one can read epics that illuminate the thoughts and replenish the faith.

Shadow of the Future

The smell of frankincense aromatizes the hallways flowing incessantly from the bride's quarters. There I see the royal retinues dressing in their fanciest gowns and hurrying with the golden bowls of honey and oil. And the bride smiles at dawn by the window of her intricate bedroom awaiting her anointment with romantic anxiety. To her, the future has become a mission of excitement, an exploration of love, life, children, success, and more.

A prosperous life she and her prince shall have, enhanced by the birth of their offspring and enriched by the crown of love, loyalty, and heroism.

The prince on the other side of the palatial building foresees his own future. Standing on the grand balcony outside his quarters, he contemplates life and its adventures. And the mysteries of the unknown dance with the somber clouds of autumn only to rejuvenate his endeavors and reinforce his confidence. On his wedding night, he awaits his bride with a moving calmness and a serene devotion.

Suddenly, a dark shadow overwhelms the skies above and beyond and flows toward the prince. Thunder scrapes the skies, shakes the earth, and makes the large stone walls of the immense palace tremble. And there stretches forth a long, dark arm, the limb of a ferocious beast, which seizes the handsome prince and takes him away into oblivion. Unable to subdue the wind's might, the prince falls hence forth deep in the hollow ground, dark like misery itself and brisk like the feel of the cold teeth of the creatures of the inferno. Within my reach the prince is, yet I can neither save him nor can he see me. The guards do not hear me; the doors are forever locked, and the mist is further thickening in density and confusion.

Shadow of Desires

In the deepest bottom of the ground, the prince sits alone tired and grieved. He remembers the wedding where the shadows of the priests and the priestesses still pass him by. He still sees the shade of their immaculate white candles burning with the flame of love and faithfulness. And the merry sound of the wedding bells rings the tones of anguish and distress in his heart. For he will forever wonder why his life has been afflicted with the angers of the gods. Suddenly a lustrous flame overwhelms the whole atmosphere, brushing off the darkness of this world. And the brightness of the daylight stirs hope and happiness in the heart of the young prince. The mystery that overshadows his fate manifests itself by the appearance of a goddess only a few steps away from the prince. She looks at him with joy, for he is the god she awaits. A rare and unknown beauty flows from her face, sparkling just like rays of the morning sun sparkle over the universe. Carrying in her hands the elixir of eternity, she kneels at his feet, yet he remains mesmerized by her charm and beauty. "Who you are?" he asks. "I am what men have been looking for since the beginning! Love me, and you shall never suffer hatred; come to me, and you shall never be lonely. Give me your soul, and I shall grant you the life of the gods. I am the garden of your desires."

At this moment she sprinkles the earth beneath her with her godly elixir, and three beautiful roses bloom in the middle of a bare garden. Then she says: "These three roses are the gifts of the gods to men." She points at the red rose and says: "The first one you pick is the rose of victory. Smell it, for in its scent lies the sword of the heroes. It shall shine before your eyes just like wisdom shines in the temple of God. Take the sword and keep it on your side, for it is the weapon with which you will conquer your enemies, and no man shall ever live to oppose you. All the hard roads to glory that are implanted with the risks of failure will be paved for you instead with success and power. And remember that in power reside the causes of war, and from its nature stems the branches of peace."

Then she points to the pink rose and says: "This rose is

the flower of love. Pick it with your own hands and do not forget to smell it, for from its scent flourishes the kingdom of love. In this kingdom, all the goddesses of the universe will bless your life with love and ardor. They will live at your mercy and will cry for your passion. This rose is the ultimate dream of every man. With it your heart shall never be lonesome and your life shall never be longing for the charm of companionship." Then she looks at the third rose and says: "This white rose is the flower of eternity. Pick this one last and smell it deeply until its aroma penetrates your heart and beholds your being, for in its essence dwells the house of eternity. Old age, the monster that men fear, shall fear you! You shall forever remain a young monarch. You shall never hear the wailing of the old, useless souls or the caustic laughter of the young, proud souls. And the inevitable cycle of life that seizes the fate of every man can neither halt your dreams nor throw you in the dark corners of inertia and decrepitude.

Shadow of Humanity

The prince walks in the garden of his desires toward the three roses and picks them one after the other, yet he does not smell them. He looks at each one of them with joy and embarrassment—joy for feeling the world within his grasp and embarrassment for feeling the chill of sinful temptation. At this moment, he recalls the song of victory chanted years ago by his glorious father, saying:

Glory to the heroes that men's courage makes and blessed are those that die for men's sakes.

Then a shadow, so white like the clouds of heaven, passes him by. It speaks with the prince's voice, yet it has no face one can see or body one can touch. He looks at the prince and says: "Can the beauty of a goddess and the charm of a rose induce a man to sell his soul??"

"How will you ever hear the bells of victory when they peel for you at dawn?"

"How will you wear the clad of victory when your own valor did not design it?"

"How will you feel the pride of victory when your own soul did not earn it?"

"Let your endeavors build you the sword with which you conquer the enemies of man and then share your victory with your fellowmen."

"Is there life without challenge?"

"Is there victory without risks?"

"Is there power without bravery?"

"And what is bravery other than the courage of the souls and the determination of the spirit?"

"From its roots, the tree of wars and peace grow and bloom to fulfill humanity's most ecstatic needs."

After long moments of silence and contemplations, the prince recalls the song of matrimony that the angels chanted for him on his wedding night:

"Oh, Children of Earth," the song goes, "behold that devotion sanctifies love, loyalty blesses it, and commitment grows it in the hearts of men to unfold humanity's deeds—the fruit of virtue that nurtures our souls. Pure and lofty is the kingdom of love, for it resides forever under the wings of god." But the prince looks at the second rose and cries: "Is it not that in this rose hides the treasure of every man?"

"Remember," says the shadow, "that it is the eyes of man that edify the rose, his spirit that tenderizes its petals, and his senses that recognize its fragrance."

"You who are tempted are human. But you who break under temptation are a weak and breakable being. For you have no will to resist, no heart to survive, and no virtue to crown your manly promises."

"Taste the pleasure in the warmth of the woman who cherishes your soul yet does not own it, who holds your life with strength and dedication yet keeps you free on the face of the Earth, who bears the children in her womb yet gives them your name and the name of your forefathers to keep you, ungrateful man, living in the hearts of the future generations."

"I say that she who ages with you in wisdom and accomplishments is she who holds the key to your eternal life."

"Without her tears, you shall be thirsty."

"Without her smile, you shall be lonely."

"Without her charms, you shall never reside in the comfort of companionship."

"Is there love without sacrifice? Is there happiness without suffering?"

"Climb the ladder of ethic; you will find it hard and troublesome, yet you shall reap honor."

"Descend the road of temptation. You find it smooth and effortless, yet you shall reap deception and shame."

Then the prince cries again: "But the rose offers me eternal life."

And the shadow answers: "There shall be no life without death. There shall be no death without eternal existence!"

"Do not fear the end; for it is only the beginning, just like childbirth bewilders your heart with joy and awe to the miracles of life, thus death amplifies your heart with wisdom and reverence to the secrets of life. And the cycle of life that the rose fears, I tell you live it and do not escape it or fear it. For it is only fear that makes you succumb to the treacherous empty world of unfulfilled promises. There men live the life of snakes crawling down below with their poisoned deceptions and their fatal calamities."

"I ask you, what makes men worthy?"

"I ask you, what makes men care for the seed they plant in the ground?"

"I say if the tree does not grow in years to give fruit and flavor to men, men cut the tree from the roots and throw it into the fire. And fire is the ultimate reward hidden in the rose of the sorceress."

"And the ageless prince whose life the sorceress describes with vigor and vitality? I tell you, ageless is the soul of man who excels in years to give our lives purpose and meaning. I say without the harmony of natural ascendance and progression, man becomes the forsaken being thrown into the coldness of inertia and decrepitude."

"Man the Supreme Being enters the house of divinity only after his soul gives humanity her favorite taste of substance and significance. Then the soul of man flies the heavens of life in the world of excellence, as the butterfly flies the flowers of nature mystified by the dazzles of God's inventions."

"And what is the butterfly other than the tiny worm of nature that miraculously grows to reward our lives with the splendor of silk and its exquisite softness?"

* * * * * * * * * * * * *

At this moment the goddess approaches the prince with an irresistible grace and a godly softness and says: "Smell the roses; they are yours." But the prince throws the roses under his feet, and they become three black snakes crawling down below. He turns to the goddess to speak to her, but instead he finds an ugly beast with the head of a serpent and the eyes of a human looking at him with bitterness and rage.

From its mouth flow poison and loud cries. Then the prince hears the whining of the declined and forgotten spirits erring around him in distress and torment. And the prince falls prostrate, down to the ground, and sheds excessive tears of pain and agony to humanity's corruptions. "I ask you no more," says the shadow, "for now you are prepared to ask your own self the imminent question for which you shall enjoy living, searching for an answer that abides in your deepest innermost." And the shadow and the prince reunite again, and together they walk the road of discovery.

The Shadow

It is spring, and I continue my walk through the orchards where the trees smile at the cheerful season with their most abundant flowers. There in an old vineyard, I see an aging but vigorous prince sitting by his beloved son. The young crowned prince asks his father: "Tell me, my lord, what is it that makes humanity worthy of the beatitude of life?"

The old man says: "I say mind yourself of the elixir of eternity held by the hands of whom the eyes of man love, but their souls expel in distaste for this elixir is morbid.

Let your honor be the master and your virtue the guide, for your soul is the price."

"There shall be no price for the soul of man or a reward that shares its worth. I say that the soul of man is the fragrance of humanity. Without it, man is nothing but a putrefied piece of earth, eaten by the worms of earth. I say there exists no man without a soul, a soul shall never exist without a god."

And why does a wondrous and perplexing question haunt my thoughts in the most silent segment of my life?

Why does a sheer and fine thread tie the life of this old prince to my life in moments of deep intimacy and dignity?

Though I never met the prince or saw his face before, he remains in my heart the dearest friend I shall ever have.

Chapter Four

THE REWARDS OF LIFE

"Does nature touch you if you do not worship
her sea and adore her mountains?""
"Does the fertile land render its generous crop if you do not
nurture its deepest soil with your earnest care and adherence?"

In the midst of a beautiful silent night of mystery and solitude, my long-awaited friend finally visits me. She finds me in calmness and tranquility, and I find her in pain and in tragedy, sobbing like never before. "Why in tears, my friend?" I ask. She replies with a recital that bewilders the soul and incites the imagination:

My heart is shattered
My dreams are scattered
I am doomed into oblivion
My reality shall never be born

Lonely, I am, trampled like a rose petal
Lost I wander, in the darkness of my life, looking for a candle
    that would inflame the first light of my lost hope.
My foes conquered me
They crushed my endeavors and celebrated victory
They expelled me out of the gardens of my desires into a
    thousand years of austerity!"

* * * * * * * * * * * *

My friend continues saying: Into the spacious path of existence I walk, aiming to capture the rewards of life. After a long travel, I arrive at the Garden of Children. There, laughter caresses innocence, and tenderness flows from the hearts of the gods. There the sun has a brighter light and the air a smoother feel. There the smell of the spring blossom enraptures one's senses, and the heavenly music of the season beholds one's heart. Around me a huge crowd of children whispers hymns of devotion to the fountains of paradise. The same fountains sprinkle those children's entities in the orbit of life, like pure crystal, thence they spread and grow and fill the sphere with substance and vigor. An indescribable fear mixed with streaks of joy grasp me at the sight of the group of youngsters standing in array one next to the other. They look at me intently, and I look at them softly. An inevitable feeling tells me that they are part of me. A discreet conviction tells me they are mine. Our lives communicate harmoniously, and I feel that I am reaching my reward.

I pull both hands with the most affectionate need to gather them in my arms until the youngest one abruptly exclaims: "We do not belong to you! We are what should have been yours had you yielded to the sacrifices of motherhood. We are the bridge that should have linked you to your future, but now you shall live in the future of others.

Words that pierce thru my heart are spoken by those whose resemblance to myself leaves me in a stupor. They gradually disappear behind the cloudy veil of nature, and I turn away in pursuit of my path. The echo of their songs precedes my shadow.

Standing in a desert full of thorns
A mother whose angels are never born
The beat of their pulse she hears
And their fancy holiday dresses, she adorns.

* * * * * * * * * * * *

31

My friend paused for a moment, and then went on saying: I continue my walk in an abyss of conflicting emotions of deception and penitence. With hope remaining my most loyal companion, I knock at the door of the Garden of Love. Two little angels, singing their holiest songs of creation, come forward and open the imperial gate. There, my friend, I hear psalms of Adam and Eve, of Adonis and Ishtar, and of Isis and Osiris. I see men and women chanting their sacramental fidelities under the clear and open skies of Eden. The mystifying smell of their sweet libation enchants my ailing soul to the utmost. There my eyes witness the joy of unity and learn the grace of companionship. There love attests to its divinity. There matrimony asserts the beatitude of its imminence. There commitments are sworn under the eyes of God and not through the fanciful designs of man and hypocrisy. I beg life to keep me entranced in the thrill of this symphony. I look, and my eyes clash with those of a captivating man. He stares at me as if he is reliving a long and tiring dream—a stranger to my eyes, yet he and I share a lifetime together. My heart is thirsty. My spirit is dancing. My passion seeks comfort. And I shall go to him, my awesome reward, so our lives will finally adjoin in ecstasy.

No! Says the voice so familiar that I tremble, the voice

of the woman from my hazy past who once looked up to me in envy while I look down at her with pity.

Now she looks at me with indifference, and with a chilling and poisonous voice she says:

"He is what should have been yours had your heart ever envisioned his truth."

He could have been the mercy to all sins had your eyes ever noticed the glow of his genuineness."

"He should have been the treasure to your beauty had your senses ever felt his existence."

"He could have been the warmth to your cold winter had you ever revered his humanity."

"He should have been the reality of your dreams had you ever acknowledged his endeavors."

"He could have been the foundation to your temple had you ever recognized his interest—your temple that stands beyond your swirling present, the temple of your kindred that stores your memories and perfumes them with the scent of legacy and revival. Thus, they softly ascend with the breeze of success and triumph into the skies of the forthcoming generations that arise hereafter."

I look at the woman in shock and with remorse. I open my shivering lips to sing to the prince whose crown I betrayed and whose glory I mocked the song of eminent and preserved life. But he could never hear my weak and fading voice, for the woman in white wraps him with her veil and flies with him into infinity. And I walk away from my own self, trying to escape the somber passages of deception, with the song of the two little angels becoming my only reminder of the Garden of Love.

> *A woman drifts in her search and*
> *takes pride in deprivation*
> *A woman rejoices in her return to the*
> *land of reunion and consolation*
> *A woman who glorifies arrogance and*
> *takes nobility into exaltation.*

* * * * * * * * * * * *

My good friend pauses again and continues her recital saying: I leave the Garden of Love, burnt from the fire of rejection, and I enter the Garden of Friendship where camaraderie soothes one's troubled feelings. There, I see men gathered in prayer, all in one voice and one hymn, uttering words of thanks to the lord of humanity. There, religious creeds and manmade doctrines are banished from people's thinking. There, corruptive discrimination and selfish love lose their meaning.

There, jealousy and envy disappear. There, the virtue of brotherhood and friendship become the basic tenants of all societies. I look toward the crowd that surrounds me, searching for this element of affinity that fulfills each one's life with the gifts of life.

I bestow upon them my finest supplication, asking to spend the rest of my days humming with them the tune of mankind, the song of brotherhood. But the kindest in the crowd approaches me saying: "Go back to your own land, for you have chosen to be among a breed that is not born yet. We are what exuberance has prevented you from attaining."

"We are what you have despised inside your silky and shiny covers. Our kindness disgusted you. Our chivalry spoiled you. Our loyalty bored you. Our friendship annoyed you! You are too different to belong."

They all turn away and leave, and I turn my back and walk.

Dance my soul young and lonely
Triumph my sins and catch my tears
My life hides in my shadow
My memories are cold
And I am in fear

My senses are dulled
The truth is near
Lord of forgiveness
Accept me, oblation in your deep tolerance.
There my putrefied spirit shall be aromatized with the essence
  of your humility.

* * * * * * * * * * * *

My good friend pauses again but goes on saying: I leave with the litany of truth beating on my conscience. I shall go back to where love and affection secure my existence. I shall go back home. I shall go back to my shelter. I arrive to my family house on a bright sunny day. I pass by the luxurious blue sea that kindles in my mind old recollections of merry days of childhood. There, in the old home that hides in its walls the splendor of antiquity and unity, I will rest after a long and tiresome search. There I shall hear the laughter of the spring prance around my window, watch the beauty of the summer embrace our orchards, smell autumn bless our land, and foresee the secret of winter shield our dreams. I walk toward my family, nicely sequestered in the afternoon as they exchange thoughts of wisdom and share time of laughter. Toward them I hurl with eagerness, yet by them I pass like an invisible faded creature. Suddenly

I see an aging man on whose face the lines of many years reveal their mysteries. He addresses me kindly! "You are invisible," he says, "for you do not carry in you the seeds that your parents implanted in you. Your siblings do not feel you, for you did not preserve the yeast through which life kneaded you together."

Did you weep with your brothers so they smile with you? Did you pray with them so they celebrate with you?" Then he continues saying: "You are unfair to life!"

"Does the morning sun penetrate your window if you do not open your shade?"

"Does nature touch you if you do not worship her sea and adore her mountains?""

"Do the birds sing to you their favorite melodies if you do not listen to them?"

"Does the fertile land render its generous crop if you do not nurture its deepest soil with your earnest care and adherence?"

"Does god infiltrate your heart if you do not eat his sacred bread and drink from his sacred cup?"

"But instead, you have destroyed the cup and thrown the bread to the worms of the earth, so the feet of the ungrateful man steps on the holy givings of the lord!"

"Those who enjoy the taste of honey are those who enjoy the bee's sting, and those who appreciate the beauty of the rose and adore its scent are those who welcome the alluring prickling of its pointy thorns."

"You lost yourself looking for success, yet you decline to know that success stems from sacrifice, and sacrifice springs from love, and love flows from humility, and humility resides in the center of the spirit of god! So intent you were to find conceited fame that you forgot to reap the awesome rewards of life."

The old man disappears, but his voice forever remains my only prayer for the bitter and forlorn nights.

* * * * * * * * * * * *

On this note, my friend ends her bewildering recital. I approach her slowly to offer my compassion and lend my support. But I do not see my friend, only my own reflection through the golden frames of a vast mirror. I tremble, just like the thin tree limb trembles, old and dry, bending with the graceful moves of the wind until it breaks to disembranchment. Thus, I break into endless agony. Looking at my own reflection in the mirror of wisdom, I condemn my own self into a thousand years of mourning. Between my guilty hands I hold the vestiges of my own fallen life.

What happened to whom my eyes saw as my best friend?

What will become of my life and what Garden shall I seek? There at the end of a foggy tunnel sparkles the flame of life and shines the eternal spirit of wisdom.

CHAPTER FIVE

BEYOND THE CONTINENT

"The homeland is god's treasured reward to his people.
"He who renounces the gift of god
shall be expelled from the kingdom of his ancestry"

Now life stretches its merciful arm and kindly turns the last page of the final chapter of the Book of Knowledge. For years I read the book, enduring a muddling learning experience of confusion and controversy. For a long time I awaited the end of a perplexing volume. Now I am ready to embark, find justice, and reveal to her the profanity of her faithful followers. A world cruel and pitiless is left behind; I bear no attachment to the bitter and searing pain the knife of war carves on my bleeding heart.

Here I am sailing the Ship of Fate in silence and meditation.

Success is my aspiration.

Sapience is my leading light.

Compassion is my shield.

Truth is my clad.

And the memories of the loved ones befriend my soul to clear and erase the dark passages of loneliness. And why do I turn tremulous and cold?

So engulfed I am in my remembrance that I barely notice the Great Ship sailing back to its proprietor. Finally on land, on the other side of the continent I walk astray, listening to the murmurs of the hills and plains. Standing at the foot of a mountain, I hear the soft breeze of eternity whisper fascinating and inviting stories of all ages, stories of glorious odysseys that cherish this kingdom since creation. "Here it is," the song goes, "where the legacies of love, heroism, and sanctity breathed life and fertility in the soil of a copious and high land."

I start way up en route to my destiny in a perpetual admiration of this masterpiece—the work of the Grand Artist. As I step on the acme, I feel absorbed by a heavenly pine fragrance that unfolds the blue skies of this white Elysium. And there, like the bright sun of a mid-August day, shines an angelic shadow. With superior nobility and a mysterious melancholy, he sits under an imperial cedar tree. The tree is old like those other cedars all majestically standing one next to the other, as if their sole intent is to crown the whole mountain with a firm commitment and a brave determination. Old indeed, yet rejuvenating with their emerald green branches, each time a desirous foot sends threatening signals on the borders of this fortress.

I remain imbued by the charm of the shadow whose face I am unable to see, yet his preponderant magnificence captures my moments.

Thoughts swirl in my mind about the shadow, his name, his origins, and his purpose!

And swiftly, like the speed of the butterfly toward the blooming flower, a vigorous yet melodic voice addresses me with serenity: "My name is Luban," he says with an unprecedented pride and grandeur.

"I am the son of this mountain. Here is my birthplace and in here I shall dwell forever. "My purpose is to keep the name of this land eternally pure, and on this mount, I must withstand all the injustices of the world."

"Luban," I say, "the fancy of all nations. To you Europe sang her holiest song of recognition:

The sea of Luban
The blue Jewel

The Groom of all civilization
The shore of Luban
The founder of modern alphabet
The parent of the color of love
Red, the bright symphony
The loved child of every artist
The sweet rose of every romantic"

"My blue sea," he angrily cuts in, "is boiling with the blood of my contending children." And there he speaks in lament:

"I am the one whose sons desert their kingdom to live in slavery."

'They abandon the aroma of incense to hide in the corners of lucrative industries."

"I am the one whose heart my children ripped into thousands and thousands of pieces."

"They trade their dignity with the wealth of the conqueror."

"They sell their heritage to the highest bidder."

"With the blade of the sword they split and tarnish my white cape so each one of them could freely enjoy my kingdom in independence."

"Independence?" I ask "Independence", he replies, "is the height of human ascendance, a very sophisticated phenomenon. People with valor and worth earn it and

die for it so the flame of liberty kindles thereafter."
"Independence, my son," he says, "is the river that flows
from liberty. And liberty is what those cedars stood for
since time immemorial!"

"Those brave men", he continues "that ushered
independence into this era fought the greed of ruthless
empires to preserve the autonomy of their motherland.
But these men, who shamefully twist the legacy of their
predecessors, are warring in their own backyard, father
against son and brother against brother. When their fight
reaches the inescapable end, they will be left with no
autonomy and no identity. Like a tree that has no roots,
they shall become men with no origins, no state, no national
merit! Refugees they will be in their own entity. Miserably
they will wander forever strangers and traitors in the house
of independence."

His sadness touches my heart. Why do Luban and I
share an indelible grief?

I turn and look beyond the spacious continent. I
call on the free men of this age who satiate Earth with
mankind's favorite articles of international laws and world
responsibilities! I call on you, crusaders of civilizations,
sponsors of humanity's inalienable rights! Why do you
throw your most sacred banner into oblivion?

Why does the wicked obsession of all times freeze your hearts and mask your minds?

The ultimate obsession with power and supreme influence.

Silence befalls the forest of the cedars. Luban, tired yet tenacious, looks at me and protests: "You read the book of knowledge, yet you fail to recognize the mother that bore you."

You learn the realities of others, yet you fail to conceive your own truth."

"Read the pages that your own mind inscribes; be master of your own destiny. Then, and only then, you obfuscate confusion and destroy all controversies."

"You sail miles away looking for justice, yet you do not search for it in your own midst."

"From the abyss of your own wisdom justice stems, just like men spring from the breath of God"

"The scar that the war leaves on your own heart is the design of your own betrayal."

"And the free men you accuse of the wickedness of all times you worship".

"Open your vision and close your eyes; you see these men dining at your children's and grandchildren's tables."

"Your success failed you, and your sapience had no light."

"Your compassion gave you away, and your truth stripped you from reality."

I lean forward to touch Luban and celebrate our reunion with him, but instead I find myself miles away, back in the same town where I joyfully celebrated before departure.

I am in the middle of a busy crowd, standing with a black book in one hand, a cedar wood pencil in the other hand, and perfumed incense flowing everywhere. To the Ship of Fate I appeal:

Take me back to Luban. I want to kiss his feet and drown in the softness of his passion.

Take me back to implore forgiveness from the land that opened my eyes to the gifts of god, shaped my dreams, and stirred my hopes.

Take me back to the land of prodigies—the fountain of culture and knowledge. Take me back to the land of the prophet who fascinated the world with his famous message of love, marriage, and children; the prophet who sculpted Luban's glory in every corner of the world; the prophet who kept the lamp of our lives lit!

Take me back. Do not let me die in isolation. For I am a lonely and sad old being whose ashes belong to the dust of the land of the cedars, and to this dust I shall return.

Take me back to the land that gave me my first

inspiration. There, in the bosom of my mother, my soul shall rest in peace and integrity.

I want my spirit to reside in the antiquity of my forefathers' village and my shadow to warm its old ecstatic walls.

I want my tears to moisten the soil of my ancestors' orchards and my endeavors to blossom with the fruit of their hard work.

I want the sea of Phoenicia to anoint my body and its waves to cleanse my conscience.

I want to be in the land where I could kneel to the consecrated beauty of nature and witness absolute perfection embrace absolute reality."

"Take me back o ship of fate," I say. But I only hear the echo of my shattered voice.

At last the kind arm of life opens the beginning segment of my book. On its first page I lay down my opening sentence:

The homeland is god's treasured reward to his people. He who renounces the gift of god shall be expelled from the kingdom of his ancestry.

* * * * * * * * * * * * *

Back in the land of nowhere, I set sail.

Independence is my direction.
Liberty is my power.
Justice is my faith.
Loyalty is my essence

And the memories of the beloved ones consolidate my contemplations and wrap my heart, so I sustain myself intact to the sins of forgetfulness. And why do warm, grievous tears pour in abundance while my heart cries, yet my eyes are arid and thirsty?

CHAPTER SIX

A DREAMING SOUL

"You shall need no water, for now you drink the nectar of life."
"You shall need no bread, for now you eat the fruit of life."
"You shall need no clothing, for now you wear the awe of life."

In our quest for discovering how real our reality is and how concrete our faith is, we must continue the journey of discovery, seeking a pure destination free from illusions and deceptions. Perusing the epics of many centuries has been a perpetual dream. Finally, we resolve to take the trip of discoveries. We will look for the divinity of life in a world where the very essence of life is questioned and rejected by many who feel that the divinity of life no longer offers substance in a universe full of great inventions.

Our excitement grows while we travel, and our anticipation grows as we approach our destination, just within reach of the world of knowledge. In the midst of our celestial reveries, we hear the angels of our dreams hum blissful melodies in a heaven that seems so real. Farther into our walk, we begin hearing mystical melodies echoing in the background. We hear the psalms of all psalms:

"You shall need no water, for now you drink the nectar of life."

"You shall need no bread, for now you eat the fruit of life."

"You shall need no clothing, for now you wear the awe of life."

While traversing the path of discovery, we reach many cities and cross many lands. We see crowds of people wandering. Others are searching, and yet more are celebrating life and its mystery. Suddenly, we pass a large and elevated temple. In its center, we see a working man adding the final stones to an erect building. Walking toward him, we wonder how a man stricken with blindness can cut the stones of nature with precision and adjoin them with art when he is unable to see the work of his own hands. With command and assertiveness, the old hermit questions our thoughts, saying:

"I ask you, does the child of humanity need eyesight to design the altar of worship? Or is faith what he needs to envision the temple of worship?

"Does he need eyesight to build the structure of faith,

or is spirit what he needs to assemble the temple of the son of faith?"

Wondrous questions of faith, mind, and spirit, for which we have no answers, come from this man. We never knew him, and yet his tone sounds so familiar. From the beginning, we meant to avoid getting lost in a labyrinth, and yet it looks as though we have lost the direction of the path. A hermit standing on the steps of the temple that arches over the ages and extends across the centuries speaks to us as if he knows us, and yet we do not know him. Could he be the guardian of the path? A perplexing type of fear befalls us as we remain by the temple, looking at the man and wondering whether we should move forward or go back.

With ease and masterly intelligence, the old hermit answers, "Focus on your destination, and you will not be lost."

Are we not focused on our destination? we ask ourselves.

"You may be focused on the destination but not on the purpose of your voyage," the hermit replies. "I tell you, there are many roads, many paths, and a million curves on the way to your destiny. By mistake, you may take an unintended trail. But you will still reach your destination if you remain focused on the purpose of it all.

"Without destination, life loses its significance. And without clarity of purpose, a person cannot reach his or her objective; he or she will endlessly question the path, battling fears and doubts and losing the direction of the whole voyage." The hermit goes on, "As for who I am, I am the child of humanity whose heart is guided by the light of faith and empowered by the soundness of spirit.

"I am the people of the old, the new, and the forthcoming ages.

"And as for who you are, you are the people of today, the generation that achieved some milestones of progress but, unfortunately, could not stay the course to progress.

"You are looking for faith, but somehow you doubt my very existence even as we are having this conversation.

"You are the people who enjoy the expansive gifts of modern education—of science, history, philosophy, and so much more—yet reject substance, retaining the veneer that keeps you questioning even the truth of your own selves.

"Then you resolve to travel great distances looking for the substance of faith and the proof of reality while faith and reality are manifest in the spirit of your own life.

"Faith eludes you, for you do not grasp its essence. Embrace the essence of faith to earn its joy with no illusion."

THE ORATION OF FAITH

"How can one grasp the meaning of faith?" one of us asks.

The hermit responds, "Only with the good sense of logic will you feel the living vibration of faith. It is only by welcoming its sensation that you will be able to absorb the meaning of faith.

"Today, faith has been isolated. It is labeled as the enemy of logic, intellect, and reason. Therefore, you lose feeling for it. Yet no second of life could pass without the inspiring touch of faith working its mystery to complete and fulfill every single act of logic, intellect, and reason.

"I tell you that faith is one wholesome energy transmitting a distinct and infinite message in every simple, ordinary, and touchable aspect of each instant we live. Thus it penetrates the field of my senses and permeates the touchable world, flowing beyond the boundaries of everything vivid and concrete that defines my human existence. And so I feel the work of faith as it restores belief in what I see and ushers truth to what I envision. Fostered by the greatness of the spirit, faith flows in abundance to complete and fulfill the highest moments of our existence.

"I tell you, faith, if rejected, leaves a void in one's life. So many of you today search to fill faith's place with entities outside its realm and utterly external to its sphere and domain.

In consequence, you wander infinitely. You stroll astray, looking for the thrill of fulfillment while really rejecting it, deviating from the path and dissolving the purpose.

"I tell you, look for faith by engaging the mind's reason. Reach for it in the depth of your soul, for it is ingrained in the nucleus of humanity by the spirit of being that links us to the gates of eternity.

"I tell you, without faith I could never envision the temple, foresee its design, and put forth its structure. In the silence of my thoughts, I reach to my mind. In the intensity of my prayers, I seek my inner self. Ultimately, I will allow my whole being to capture the substance of faith in the greatness of the spirit.

"Sadly, today the phenomenon of faith is being rejected as obsolete, nonexistent, and fictional.

"I tell you, faith is part of the essence that composes humanity. It has been part of you since birth, like every part of your body and soul. How could you reject a part of yourself?

"Sadly, today the very foundation of faith is relentlessly scrutinized by a system of thinking that is confined to the world of concrete. It insists that what is there is there, and there is nothing beyond what the eyes see.

"I tell you, faith works in the field of the mind and the

depth of the spirit. Without it, there is no possibility of anything concrete, solid, or true. I say, behind every solid substance lies an invisible energy working within you and outside of you to finally manifest itself to the eye. It is this magnificent energy that allows you to see the clear and the solid, the real and definite. This substantiates the power of the invisible in the world of reality.

"Today, you forget that every act of assertion and every notion of acknowledgment comes as a result of an involuntary act of faith. Man denies this and seeks to illogically analyze all manifestations of faith in all of its shapes and forms.

"I tell you, remember that doubt is a natural phenomenon in the working of human reasoning. To doubt is not to disbelieve or reject. Embrace the pulsation of faith while you float in the natural phenomenon of doubt, for with every episode of disbelief the mind grows in multiple dimensions, aiming at discovering layers of reality in the fields of life. Do not lose sight of the purpose while glancing through the many chapters of disbelief, lest you drift, get lost, and never reach your destination.

"I ask you, how will you ever reach to the mind if you have no faith in its existence?

"How will ever trust your mind if you have no faith in its substantive reality?

"In the soundness of the mind, the exquisite logic of faith is kindled. In the mystique of faith, the mystery that shields reality is unveiled. That is how the real becomes evident: by the strength of logic and the work of faith in the depth of our thoughts.

"I tell you, do not isolate faith, for it is a great gift to the field of thoughts.

"Be aware of the method you employ in your search, for the method is pertinent to the truth. Today, you look for the truth by exploiting science to explain existence. But science is nothing more than a simple phenomenon in the field of life. It is invented by the minds of men and women, but existence is the science of God spelled out in a reality that originates in the essence of the soul of men and women.

"Use the method of reason, empowered by the keenness of the mind, to discover the power of faith. Remove the blindness from your vision and approach the archway of existence. Thus you will empower your search by employing a clear, compelling, and potent method.

"That is how I design the temple in my mind. With fervent faith I built it, for I am the hermit who sees the daylight spring from the gloom of blindness as clearly as I see the reality of the beatitude of life.

"I tell you, through the vast sea of life glides the glory of faith. From mystery and uncertainty, the greatest of human minds ascertain the reality of god."

* * * * * * * * * * * *

We stand at the bottom of the thousands of steps to the grand temple, taking a moment to discern the message of the hermit. His words sink deeper into our minds, his soul touches our hearts, and we begin feeling the bliss of our encounter. We burn with fear and courage. Our encounter with the hermit, his candor about the fundamentals of his thinking, his search, his resilience, and his vulnerability outline the map of our voyage in the divinity of life. It is at this very moment that the hermit speaks again, saying,

"You are indeed seeking the solidity of what your heart feels, but your eyes are unable to see. You are searching for the truth that your eyes see, but your mind is unable to define.

"I tell you, dive into the sensuous dynamics of knowledge, and immerse yourself in the glory of faith. Allow your eyes to see the feelings of the heart, and allow your mind to define the truth that floats in the sight of the naked eye. Keep both mind and faith in their proper sanctuary. Otherwise, they wander lost as displaced entities in the shallowness of life, detached and unaware."

We are drawn to the fluency of the hermit's reflections. He painstakingly attunes himself to the embryonic stage of our developing thoughts. It is not by simple coincidence that we met the hermit. It is by our unrelenting persistence in seeking the answers of life through years of painful voyages laden with the tears of deception and the cries of failure. Answers come now multifold, glorifying our previous failures and celebrating our future endeavors. Here our failures turn into cherished lessons, which we value for the years of wandering they hold in each chapter, each page, and each utterance. Now we edge toward celebrating a clear reality through the keen senses of an acute and unadulterated faith. The hermit continues his talk, eloquently reasserting, "With my spirit, I assemble the temple of faith. With fervor, I celebrate the living proof of the son of faith."

SPIRIT

The hermit goes on in a lengthy discourse of exultant thoughts, saying:

"In the exquisite fabric of the spirit, the realm of faith and the field of mind are magically interwoven.

"I cherish my spirit for its ability to capture the substance of faith, and I pursue the thrill of faith to cultivate my spirit.

"Thus, with uncompromising faith, I design the temple. With unwavering spirit, I assemble it.

"I tell you, never let your spirit falter, for it is the fuel that injects life into your veins. It is the energy that stokes your will with power. It is the bliss that gives you strength and comfort, taking you beyond perceptions and discernment to defeat hesitations, fears, and disbeliefs. It travels with you to the heights of faith. Thus you shall persist, and thus you shall learn.

"It is the force that must not be isolated, ignored, or questioned. Embrace it with the simplicity of the child and the maturity of the sage.

"I say, the spirit is the vessel of truth, the wellspring of our essence, the house of our souls, and the guardian of our identities. It is indeed the dwelling in which we exist wholesomely. In the center of this great entity dwells the seed of faith. Look deep into yourself, and submerge the workings of the mind into the depth of the spirit. Behold the seed, and plant it in the roots of your thoughts. It will bloom in all the seasons of the years and fill the days of your life with reality and divinity.

"I tell you, men and women who isolate their minds from the spike of the spirit are victims of their own injudiciousness. They are educated, and yet they remain ignorant. They acquire knowledge, and yet they are illiterate. They look, but they do not see. They read, but they do not understand. Finally, they conclude that the spirit is a myth of the past. They decide it is in the domain of the intangibles, obsolete and irrelevant in the world of today and the reality of tomorrow.

"They make amazing scientific discoveries, developing automated functions and grand electronic technology, and they move with speed and excellence. Yet they fall prey to their own inventions, as if they have become the servants of their own creations. That is how they obfuscate the reality of their beginnings, their origin, and their essence. Men and women create laws, formulas, and scientific equations, so how can it be that science turns around to be the creator of men and women?

"Thus men and women falter in their understanding. Thus they betray the nucleus of their essence, lose track, and stutter with the truth. They spend years researching the history of creation to find "themselves" while their selves are right there in the deepest depths of their own betrayed spirits.

"I truly tell you that mind and spirit are components of the being, intertwined and inseparable. One must accompany the other in the journey of life. The mind floats incessantly in the boundless sphere of the spirit. Together, they complete the wholesomeness of the self. Disregard for either entity leads to imbalance, discomposure, and chaos. One assists the other; each in its distinct role renders balance and unity to the self. Foster both to engage in the intricacies of life, to enhance awareness, and to free yourself from the perplexities of doubt, fear, and hesitation.

"Mind and spirit both submerge to restore strength, knowledge, and rationality to one another as two entities in one being. Then the world of intangibles becomes a livable reality in the world of tangibles. I tell you, the latter can never be without the first. The latter is always preceded by the first. Thus faith shines, solidifying the proof of being, the beauty of life, and the joy of existence in the world of tangibles and intangibles.

"I tell you, it is the strength of the spirit that helps your mind conquer the ordeals of hesitations and the tormenting nightmares of uncertainties. In its climatic gleam, the spirit elevates itself to the highest level of reason. The glory of the unseen world becomes clear and indisputable, demonstrated by our existence in the life we live. That is reality, sound and clear!

"Be aware of the error of today, which misinterprets the value of the mind, diminishing its great responsibilities in the realm of the spirit. Do not smother your thoughts in the bounds of false interpretations: thus you mire the greatness of the mind in the wastes of misguided science. Remove the boundaries and launch your mind on its quest for spiritual sagacity.

"Only by engaging yourself to your fullest potential, can you cherish you spirit, nourish it, and cultivate it.

LIFE

"I tell you, remove the obstacles that block your understanding of the simplicity of life.

"You listen to me now consumed by analysis, which renders you indifferent to understanding. You worry about what comes first, what to look for next, and what is the metric measure of every word in every sentence. The essence of life is not meant to be analyzed word by word but rather to be grasped in the overall meaning of our thoughts, which should be in a state of continuous awareness of transcendent questions and discoveries. Understand first, before you drown in the irrelevancies of analysis.

"I say life is never intended to be explored, found, and grasped in the palm of your hand. It is not to be dissected and analyzed through the laws of one discipline and the equations of another. Life, and you, are above the visual; both of you float in findings that are beyond advanced and futuristic. Uphold the intellect of the mind by acknowledging its vital role in the dominion of the spirit. Understand that the spirit at work is a revolutionary entity, supremely evolving to bestow stability and balance on your entire body of thinking and feeling. Then read the book of life and understand its terms of being, using the glossary of faith and the lexicon of the spirit.

"Practice patience, tolerance, and humility in your search, for it is lengthy. Be tenacious while climbing the heights of knowledge, for patience may elude you, and thus you may drift. Be patient, for in your patience you will acquire a multitude of answers and a mass of knowledge. Then you will grasp the matter of life, which is real and solid.

"Be aware of conceit and narcissism clouding your mind in your quest. Do not use the marvels of progress to unravel the enigmas of existence. Although progress is the proof of our success, it will remain only a small equation in the cosmos of life. Remember how the father of all wisdom humbled himself to show men and women the humility of God and the reality of the heavens.

"Remember how his awe shined to reveal the ultimate truth to all men and women. His truth taught us how the past, the present, the future, and the world beyond are all part of one grand eternity. It is one world with many lives and an eternity with many worlds.

"Look at how the everlasting light of wisdom spread its wings throughout the ages, in ancient and modern times, to unveil the wonders of faith in the heavenly abode of the saints.

"I say you need not live the life of a hermit, denounce the life of pleasantries, or practice isolation to savor the simplicity of life, pursue reality, and achieve faith in the truth that surrounds you. Just recover your spirit and launch your mind to restore to yourself what you have forfeited.

* * * * * * * * * * * * *

We listen to the hermit, painstakingly enthused by his wisdom and entranced by the depths of his thoughts, the eloquence of his words, and the simplicity of his style. He discerns the complexities of life with ease, tackling inexorable questions of existence. We listen carefully, trying to savor the meaning of each utterance in a world of mounting conflict, skepticism, and uncertainty. Though inebriated with our audience with him, we cannot escape a feeling of sadness for the world today and its struggle with adversities. In the midst of intensified unrest and disturbance, the people of today are struggling for survival, seeking safety before food and shelter before water. Should sacred, philosophical, and essential questions become less essential in a world where nations are rising against nations, citizens against citizens, regions against regions, religions against religions, and workers against workers? In the center of it all, where does the message of the hermit fit in? Here we ask ourselves: Are we looking for something that is not needed today in our world? Should we be shifting our priorities and abandoning the search? The years spent thinking about the beginning and the end; the exhausting days and nights devoted to wondering about the connection between the world of life on earth and the sphere of godly eternity; the time spent searching for the reality, the truth, and the solidity of faith—are not those questions pertinent to our lives and the essence of our existence, in peace and freedom? Are they not pivotal to the essence of relationships, be they political, social, or economic?

Suddenly we hear the stentorian voice of the hermit saying:

"I am the mystery of reality; the voice of the past; the echo of the present; and the shadow of life, death, and the future. I am the blind man who sees.

"Look deep into the mystery of being. You will see eternity dancing like an elegant swan in the cradle of every newborn.

"Enjoy the gift of being. Live every moment of your life thoroughly, rigorously, and intelligently to be able to define its purpose and embrace existence.

"Enjoy the self-questioning litany of wondering who you are and why you are here, but do not fall into the trap of denouncing the essence of your identity, the purpose of your being, and the solidity of your spirit. Do not falter in searching for the answer; it is faith in yourself that ever leads you to grasp the reality of existence in the spirit of being!

"I tell you, in the depth of our daily occurrences rests the answer of today and the vision of tomorrow.

"Hatred, greed, war, and peace are vices of the past, the present, and the future; one must treat them with concern but be fully aware that the light of wisdom shines uninterrupted throughout the ages. Do not stop asking the questions or halt the voyage of light, for in doing so, you are faltering, doubting, and surrendering your freedom to the will of others.

"Let politics take care of itself and let wars fight themselves, for your focus must remain on the worthiness of the cause even in the midst of warfare and hostility. Stay the course to reach destiny; do not abandon your endeavors.

"Political differences and fights for a multitude of causes are not to stop humanity from being human. Otherwise, the evil of man and woman would fester incessantly.

"I tell you, it only suffices to exert command and maintain control over oneself. One sound entity surpasses kingdoms of evils. One whisper of virtue eliminates worlds of darkness.

"Value human progress with depth to reap the rewards of its worth at its best. For in misunderstanding the concept of progress, you will face erroneous convictions, falling back from the substance of logic. Thus, you equate modernization with corruption, freedom with anarchy, class with immoderation, fashion with absurdities, change with chaos, tolerance with immorality, and so much more. For ignorance disguises itself in the name of many virtues, pounding on you and dragging you to follow the sweep of things, pressuring you not to question the tone of the day lest you become an outcast in your own home. Human progress is thus destroyed. As men and women advance in one aspect, they regress in others. Hence the imbalance rises in the lives of humans, be they leaders, citizens, or others from all walks of life. The void creeps in, the search begins, and the wandering starts. Fulfillment keeps escaping.

"Remain intact and immune to these errors, for it takes only a few to champion existence and save humanity. Likewise, it takes little for corruption to spread and disseminate itself, resulting in the destruction of civilizations.

"Hold fast to your spirit, for it is the power that illuminates your life with the light of knowledge, the vigor of faith, and the keenness of mind.

* * * * * * * * * * * *

In the abundance of the hermit's thoughts, we continue our climbing the steps of the temple until we finally reach the last one. The voice of the hermit still resonates with clarity, cutting through the stones of the centuries. Though he speaks like a great teacher answering thousands of questions, we remain embattled with a million other inquiries. How can one assess the hermit's pronouncement of faith, his chronicle of time, and his account of reality? We feel rebuked and guilty, for our errors are many and their gravity is great. How will we ever regain life in its fullness? The feeling of being adjudicators of our own follies is sharp, but more acutely painful is the sentencing of ourselves to indefinite punishment. Drowning in a state of hopelessness, we lament the fact that we have traveled, enjoyed, learned, and discovered but found a cruel reality.

The skies of nature shine brightly, illuminating the entire temple with dazzling radiance. We enter the temple to see opulent altars with incandescent alcoves of beauty and appeal. It is a magnificent land. We reach a world covered by the skies of heaven and decorated by cluster of gardens that grow in the care of a loving mother earth.

In our revelry, we hear once more the echo of humanity reverberating in the spacious halls of the temple:

"Finding a cruel reality is the bliss of the voyage! The only cruelty is in your condemnation of your own selves. I tell you, the honor of the search is in locating the truth. Imperfect though it may be, you must sprinkle it with the lessons of life and cleanse it with the spirit of being.

"Remember the spirit that struggled in turmoil for centuries? I say you lost hope in him.

I truly tell you that the disturbed spirit will find a lasting comfort, for the king of peace chose to find it at the peak of its anger and at the crux of its confusion.

"I say one should not have to abandon one's endeavors to capture the essence of life. The wealthy man can embrace his success with pride and enjoy the fortune of his hard work, but he must be careful not to let his soul become the captive of withering glories. Thus, he would commit his being to the suffering of internment and unceasing unrest. But I confidently say his spirit will find rest, for he enters the battle of peace within his own self.

"And the woman who was the captive of her own ambitions? I truly see her becoming free from her torment. She will reunite with what she calls the rewards of life. The errors of success are involuntary, but the decision to search for the worthiness of life is a choice willed by wisdom.

"Remember Sodom and Gommorah? I say you lost

hope for those two cities. I truly tell you that those two cities are still standing, for they chose to remain in search of the civilization of the children of God. Progress and development must not derail humanity from the path of life but instead inspire them to navigate the path of men and women to excellence. That is how humanity is served, and that is exactly how civilizations grow.

"Remember the prince who struggled to restore nobility and virtue to his kingdom?

I tell you, this is not the end of his struggle. To sustain the nobility of virtues, he must fight a never-ending battle with his self. Indeed, he will emerge the ultimate winner, the decorated hero of imminent and eminent wars.

"And the lonesome wanderer? You condemned him to a indefinite solitude. But I tell you that he will reach the climax of nationhood, independence, and freedom the moment he wakes up to a reality devoid of the essence of his history. In his wandering, he will learn from the joy of coping and reunite with himself in peace and comfort.

"Humanity is continuously searching for itself, ever looking for faith in a doubted reality and longing for a reality in the haziness of faith. In the course of this unceasing search, men and women struggle through the unfolding pages of a simple life to restore to humanity the nucleus of its essence, for mind, faith, and spirit, no matter how tested they are, will join together in their true abode."

On this note, the hermit ends his talk. Why is it that each time we get close to the answer, it escapes us? Here we are in the midst of this great temple, feeling that we have crossed an eternal universe. What does the meaning of our search become in all of this? We set out looking to capture knowledge, to find the validity of faith, and to ascertain the reality of being. But how can we quantify knowledge, and how can we measure the substance of our findings? For knowledge remains a reservoir of phenomena, never fully amassed but forever pursued. Its magnificent thrill is in seeking, not obtaining; this is in the art of learning!

We leave the temple refreshed and revived. In our quest for the divinity of life, we feel gratified by our magnificent discovery. Now we travel empowered and enriched. We are empowered by the soundness of a clear and solid reality and enriched by the manifestation of an evident and omnipresent eternity. The two real worlds are so intimately connected. They are a million years away and yet easy to reach. It is true that between the simplicity of reality and the mystique of eternity lies a hidden world of discoveries—physical, true, and factual—connecting eternity to every part of our daily lives. There lies a multitude of answers to a million years' worth of inquiries. We bid farewell to the shoals of our doubts and move forward, contemplating the immanence of faith in a sound and inescapable reality.

www.ingramcontent.com/pod-product-compliance
Lightning Source LLC
Chambersburg PA
CBHW020344290526
45785CB00005B/2159